Bar/Bat Mitzvah:

The Truth You Were Never Told

The Meaning of Mitzvah

By: Ariel Adam

Bar/Bat Mitzvah: The Truth You Were Never Told - *The Meaning of Mitzvah*
by Rabbi Ariel Adam Sholklapper

Self-Published
Los Angeles, California, United States of America

ISBN: 979-8-9925143-1-5

This is a work of fiction. Names, characters, places, and incidents are products of the author's imagination or are used fictitiously. Any resemblance to actual events, locales, or persons, living or dead, is entirely coincidental.

Cover and Interior Design by Ariel Adam Sholklapper

Printed in the United States of America
First Edition

For permissions, contact:
info@ravariel.com

Table of Contents

"You don't have to do anything to reach God, to reach enlightenment, to awaken. There is no one who can take you to God. Whoever says they will take you to God is a liar, because you are already there. There's only one living being, and want it or not, resist it or not, effortlessly you are with God already."

-Don Miguel Ruiz.

DEDICATION

This book is dedicated in loving memory of Raquel Abecassis Kassin, sister of Aron Abecassis. May her memory be a blessing.

With deep gratitude, this work is made possible through the generosity of the Aron and Shontal Abecassis Charitable Fund.

I want to give special thanks to Aron for his support, vision, and unwavering commitment to preserving and sharing the richness of Jewish tradition. He has empowered a new generation to embrace and perpetuate the values of our tradition.

PROLOGUE

"Not-knowing can be the doorway to true knowing." -Sanaya Roman

I am a trained and ordained rabbi.

I know much and, at the same time, very little. There's so much mystery hidden in this universe - what we perceive is but a fraction of what is and is not possible. To think or believe otherwise is delusion.

As I think, synthesize, envision, and write this guide to the 613 mitzvot, I pray for wisdom: to feel, see, and express a vision for Jewish practice that is nourishing, guiding, and enriching.

May I convey the possibilities, the hidden gems, within the religious practices while gently setting aside the parts that are no longer relevant.

May my love and connection to The Source Of All Life shine through. May it reach the hearts and souls of all those who need guidance to reconnect and connect with the Divine within themselves and in all things.

What does becoming a Bar/Bat Mitzvah mean? This book is here to answer that and more. *To simplify, I'll use Anita Diamant's term B-Mitzvah, a contraction of the phrase bar or bat mitzvah.

A few questions you'll find answered are: What is a mitzvah? What types of mitzvot are there? How could mitzvot enhance your life?

INTRODUCTION

B-Mitzvah is often thought of as a rite of passage, marking the transition into adulthood. However, many mistakenly equate this milestone with the ability to read a Torah portion, chant the Haftara, or recite prayers. While these tasks are important, they are not the essence of what it truly means to become a Mitzvah-observant adult in the Jewish tradition.

In fact, the Lubavitcher Rebbe, Rabbi Menachem Mendel Schneerson, emphasized it is far more crucial to understand and internalize the 613 commandments (the mitzvot) than to focus on the performance of a single ritual act, such as reading from the Torah. B-Mitzvah should signify that a young person has gained a foundational understanding of what it means to live a Jewish life — rooted in the commandments, ethics, and traditions that have been passed down through the generations.

It is vital that the "big celebration" of a B-Mitzvah only take place once a young person has completed the study of the Mitzvot. This approach ensures that the celebration reflects a true commitment to Jewish life, one that goes beyond surface-level rituals and rituals alone. Only through a deep understanding of these commandments can a young person step confidently into their role as an adult member of the Jewish community.

This book is an exploration of what it means to truly engage with the mitzvot, offering a roadmap to guide you from superficial observance to a life that is truly aligned with Jewish law, ethics, and values.

CHAPTER 1: WHAT DOES IT MEAN TO BE A B-MITZVAH?

One night, I sat down to dinner beside an 83-year-old Jewish man. We talked, and I mentioned I am a rabbi and writing a book about the B-Mitzvah process and the meaning of Mitzvah. His ceremony was 70 years ago, and he still had strong feelings to share with me.

He shared,

'I had a Bar Mitzvah. What a frustrating event. I learned to read and memorize Hebrew, which I didn't understand then - and, I'll be honest with you, rabbi, I still don't. The whole thing felt like an empty ceremony. It felt like I was paying social respect on my parent's behalf. How we 'celebrated,' the preparation, and the ceremony all seemed pointless to me then and still do today.'

To be honest, I agree with him.

I'm a rabbi, so I know I am probably supposed to find some way to justify the whole thing, but I can't. I've tried.

I told him the ceremony can carry much more meaning than it has until now, but it doesn't. Not the way it is today - nor how it was for him.

As a rabbi in a synagogue, I was bothered by the whole structure. What are we teaching? There's so much more to this moment, but we're focused on the wrong things. In some way, the B-Mitzvah ceremony is a small example of the synagogue system. From my conversation with that 83-year-old man, I'm not the only one frustrated. The problem runs deeper than the way B-Mitzvahs are structured.

He asked me, 'What can we do to make Judaism and synagogues more exciting? It seems like every generation has moved further and further away.'

He's right. There's a problem.

I don't think Judaism needs to be more exciting; it needs to be more helpful. Jewish wisdom and tools can truly enrich people's lives. The synagogue must become a place where those tools are shared, contemplated, and refined to help people navigate life. The synagogue must become a place where you can get the tools to overcome life's challenges and mitigate inevitable difficulties.

Despite how it is, the meaning and importance of B-Mitzvah can run much deeper than what it looks like.

Reinvigorating how we engage in the Mitzvah system can be the cornerstone of a more compelling Judaism.

Uncovering the gems within could become a milestone for a rich, life-long spiritual discovery process.

First, we will describe what currently exists. Then, we will talk about the actual meaning of the moment. After that, we will uncover how you can access the treasure chest of Jewish wisdom and use its jewels to guide how you build your life.

In case you don't make it to the end of this very short book, here's the spoiler.

The ideal B-Mitzvah would teach you not only what the historic mitzvot are but also how to access your Divinity, to see and feel it within yourself and in everything. You would learn to access The One referenced at the end of the Shma - The Ehad - אחד. It's only by accessing your Divine power and consciousness that you can truly live a life guided by the ever-unfolding mitzvot.

When planting a garden, you first have to decide what results you want. Which flowers, fruits, and plants do you hope for? Using the garden metaphor - What kind of feelings and realities do you wish for in your life? How do you want your life to feel? Peaceful. Joyous. Loving. Satisfying. Abundant. Exciting. Fulfilling.

It's only by knowing the results you seek and the signs of progress that you can test and see if you are headed in the right direction.

Rites of Passage

You probably already know that the B-Mitzvah is one of the significant rites of passage, or lifecycle events, for Jewish people. Between birth (naming and circumcision of boys) and death, there are really only two other big ones: B-Mitzvah and Weddings.

Each of these are milestone moments that mark a change in life status.

Weddings mark an official change from single to a new couple, and B'nai Mitzvah is the beginning of the shift from child to legal adult (at least Jewishly).

What Does B-Mitzvah Look Like Today? How Does It Add Up to Becoming an Adult?

Pop quiz! Alright, kids - you're about to have your B-Mitzvah.

What does that even mean?

You've probably been told that now you're becoming a Jewish adult. Do you really believe that?

It's kind of funny, isn't it? You're 12. Or 13. You can't even legally drive a car or vote yet. Somehow, though, you're going to be considered an adult in the eyes of Jewish law.

If you are skeptical about the whole thing, I don't blame you.

You are probably busy memorizing Hebrew that you don't know the meaning of. You're probably learning or brushing up on prayers like the Shma or Kiddush and memorizing some amount of the Torah or Haftorah pronunciations - so you can recite them publicly.

You've probably got a recording you practice with - am I mostly right so far?

You may have started reading your week's Torah or Haftorah portion (they revolve around a yearly cycle) and thinking about a theme to write a sermon or Dvar Torah.

Maybe you're doing this yourself, and your parents or rabbi or both are helping you. You wouldn't be alone if they were doing most of it for you; it's really common.

I'm not saying you couldn't do it yourself, but you're just 11 or 12, right?

The family comes from out of town for some kind of gathering or party.

Your community has a tradition of big extravagant parties, maybe not. Either way, you've probably got to get some new clothes for the occasion.

Your community may require or encourage you to take on some kind of Tikkun Olam (Fixing or Healing The World) volunteering project. They may even call it a Mitzvah project.

If you're anything like me, you might be asking yourself: how does this add up to becoming an adult? Let's think about this together.

So far, we've mentioned a few elements:

-Reading or memorizing some Hebrew prayers

-Writing a sermon

-Planning a party

-Getting new clothes

-Volunteering Project

Isn't it more of an elaborate Jewish recital? How does this have anything to do with adulthood? I'm not trying to be contrary here; I really don't understand how these add up.

Let's be generous. Maybe the whole process of memorizing Hebrew, writing a sermon, doing a volunteer project, and publicly performing these rituals is a kind of training. Still, these are just some of the beginner skills you need to start the bigger 'adulting' process.

Is There Something More?

Ok, so let's say this is the kick-off of a life-long process of becoming an adult and learning how to navigate the spiritual world. I can get behind that. It's a coming-of-age moment.

That still doesn't answer anything about why we call it B-Mitzvah specifically.

Is this just another coming-of-age ceremony?

If it were, wouldn't we just call it a ShloshEsre (thirteen) or Shtemesre (twelve) ceremony?

Or is there something more to it?

CHAPTER 2: WHAT DOES THIS HAVE TO DO WITH BEING JEWISH? WHAT IS A MITZVAH ANYWAY?

I don't know what you've learned so far. It is probably fair to say you've guessed that Mitzvah is something good, or at least it should be.

Maybe you've learned it's a good deed. Perhaps you were lucky enough to have a teacher who more accurately explained that mitzvah isn't precisely a good deed but actually a commandment or law - like the Ten Commandments (Don't kill, don't steal, etc.) - each of those is a mitzvah.

If we use the classic definition, a mitzvah is a Jewish commandment, a law. If you didn't know before, now you know. These are the laws that all Jewish people are responsible for following.

613 is a significant number for you to know.

There are 613 mitzvot, or laws (mitzvot is plural of mitzvah).

Mitzvot are Jewish laws, but, as opposed to the laws or rules of your country or state, there's really no enforcement system for consequences if you don't follow them.

The exceptions are the few mitzvot that overlap with broader societal laws - like don't kill, don't steal, and others we already mentioned. That said, there are a whole lot of mitzvot that nobody is enforcing, except for maybe via guilt from your Jewish mother, like the one about not eating bacon.

You Probably Should Know What You Are Signing Up For, Right?

Not to alarm you, but traditionally, the whole idea of B-Mitzvah is that age 12 or 13 is the cutoff of when a kid becomes responsible for following the 613 mitzvot and for whatever 'Divine consequences' may come from not following the laws.

B-Mitzvah is the pivotal cutoff point, like turning 18 in the United States criminal law. After you turn 12 for girls, 13 for boys - if you committed a Jewish crime and were found guilty, you would go to adult jail instead of juvenile.

It sounds spooky, I know.

To be totally honest, I am not even entirely sure what this would mean in the Jewish context since I don't believe that's how God works, and, in most cases, there is no Jewish enforcement mechanism for these.

I can't wrap my mind around a God that is somewhere out there waiting to reward or punish us Jews for following or not following commandments, especially knowing that so many of the mitzvot are irrelevant today (as we will discuss later).

Let's add this up.

You're 12 or 13 years old and, by our societal standards, far from being an actual adult.

Your Hebrew school or day school never taught you all or even a substantial fraction of the 613 mitzvot (or even the relevant ones). And now, as you 'come of age,' you are responsible for the consequences of these laws. But you don't even know the mitzvot.

And the preparation for your ceremony only maybe, but probably doesn't/didn't, teach you the mitzvot either.

I can't help thinking about checking the 'Agree To Terms' button we all press to access apps and software. How many of us read it? Not very many of us, not entirely, at least. And yet, we agree.

Only this is different.

Clicking 'I agree' in the software/app context gives away your rights to privacy or waives your right to liability claims.

This is deeper than that, and it's not just about penalties.

It's not just about accountability to these laws.

It's about accountability to your Divine spark guidance, your intuition, the part of you that is connected to All Of Life - to God - to Love.

Moving forward with your B-Mitzvah without knowing the mitzvot is tragic.

For generations, mitzvot may have been supportive and invaluable tools.

Mitzvot have the potential to be a system that adds meaningful perspective, practices, and structure to your life.

This is worse than mindlessly clicking "Agree" in an app.

It's like clicking yes to inherit a mega trust fund, but without knowing what is in it, how to access it, or how it might massively improve your life.

If there is any wisdom at all in Judaism, its wisdom must be contained within, or in relation to, the mitzvot.

It is essential to at least know what they are or, at the very minimum, what broad categories of topics they cover.

If your ancestors transferred you a considerable trust fund, you would want to know what you had inherited.

We will go through what you've inherited together. This book/ pamphlet aims to be a categorical breakdown of the mitzvot. When you're done, you'll know the broad categories and a few examples of some specific mitzvot and how you can use them. We will explore and appraise what types of 'assets' you've inherited.

It's not just good preparation for legal accountability. It's a preparation to learn to calibrate your inner guidance. This way, you can have a better sense of the overall system. It will then be up to you to decide what interests you.

By learning the general categories, you can decide for yourself which of these treasures might make life sweeter for you or search deeper into what interests you for more specifics.

Through practice, you'll gain the skills and knowledge you need to access what already exists. You'll see how these practices flower in your life.

As time goes on, you'll evaluate - do they lead to the results you seek?

We'll also give you tools and suggestions on how to take a deeper, more granular dive if you decide that might be beneficial for your life.

We'll also try to present a vision of what mitzvah can be and how the B-Mitzvah can better prepare you for a fulfilling spiritual life.

"When you do things from your soul, you feel a river moving in you, a joy." - Rumi.

Some of the mitzvot might be interesting and helpful right away, others might be good for you later, and others may never really feel valuable to you at any point. Only time will tell.

Part of the wisdom of the tradition is that at 12 or 13, you can start to seriously grapple with how mitzvot and the tradition make sense to you as an individual.

Ideally, your B-Mitzvah is a chance to begin finding out exactly what you have inherited from your rich ancestry and to start forming your own opinions and considerations of them.

As you continue growing older and more into an actual adult, you can decide to install practices you like or want to explore and build the life you want.

This moment is an initiation to utilizing your inner guidance to navigate and discern what is relevant to, and helpful for, your life and to discovering new guidance as it arises.

The great thing is you don't need to do it all at once.

What a relief?!

Could you imagine living your entire life without ever once knowing there's a bag of treasure you inherited?

Or knowing you own one but have yet to go through it once to see what is in it or how you could make use of its gems?

That would be an absolute waste.

The rights of passage - reading the Torah, chanting Hebrew prayers, and joining in communal prayer only make sense if they follow from an understanding of the more profound wisdom they represent.

Before we dive into them, let's answer why you might care in the first place.

CHAPTER 3: WHAT'S IN IT FOR ME? WHY DO THEM?

Blasphemy is speaking sacrilegiously about God or sacred things. Is that what I've done?

I've encountered many people who say Judaism is a tradition that encourages questioning. It's not as dogmatic (a fancy word for unquestionable rules) as some other religions.

It is true that the Talmud, a central text for Judaism, records many rabbinic debates. It describes widely varying opinions on the meaning of the mitzvot and how actually to practice and uphold them.

And yet, for all the curiosity and vigorous debate, some questions are off-limits.

Technically, It Is Off-Limits to Ask This. God Says So. Whoops.

Questions like: Why practice the mitzvot? What's their purpose? In the view of many classic rabbis, it would be an unimaginable, perhaps forbidden, question to ask.

Questions like this run so counter to the basic principles of classic Judaism that they can be considered heretical.

That's because a question like this pushes against the concept that a mitzvah is a commandment from God.

As the logic goes, if God commands a mitzvah, you shouldn't need a reason or justification for why to do it; you should just do it.

The fear is that if you get overly concerned with the reasons to do or observe a mitzvah, you may only practice the mitzvot you feel have good reasons to follow or feel good and life-enhancing for you.

Where does that leave the ones that don't seem to make any clear logical sense? What about the ones that are outdated by our modern sensibilities? What about the ones that feel like they're actually making life unnecessarily harder and not enhancing our lives?

Below, I'll give a few reasons beyond 'because God said so' for connecting with, exploring, and practicing the mitzvot in your life. I will not try to defend the sort that offend me.

Connection to Ancestors

Tradition! It's something we've done for thousands of years. Our grandparents, great-grandparents, and great-great-grandparents did this: it's the way of our people.

The funny thing about this is that for all the religious debates, customs, and traditions, the most traditional thing to do is to adjust the traditions in a way that most aligns with your sensibilities. There's no single 'right' way to do that.

Practices come and go. Customs are constantly renewed, innovated, and changed.

Peter Sagal tells a jokey story on momentmag.com/jokes that illustrates this age-old debate very well:

> A synagogue is having an ongoing dispute that started small but is now getting completely out of hand. It's over whether you sit or stand during the Shema. The argument is incredibly bitter. Some people are not talking to each other. Some people are threatening to leave the synagogue unless they get their way. Family relationships have been destroyed.
>
> The rabbi doesn't know what to do, so he finds out that one of the founders of the synagogue, old Mr. Bernstein, is still alive in the Hebrew Home. He sits on the porch in a

wheelchair when the delegations for each viewpoint pay a call.

Before the rabbi can complete his opening spiel, one of the partisans bursts forth: "Mr. Bernstein, Mr. Bernstein, isn't it the tradition in our synagogue that you stand during the Shema so as to show your respect to God?" After a couple of seconds pass, he just shakes his head slightly and says, "No." So an advocate from the other side says: "So, isn't it the tradition in our synagogue that we always sit to show our humility before God?" Mr. Bernstein shakes his head and again says, "No."

The rabbi and the rest of the delegation look at each other. Finally, the rabbi says, "Mr. Bernstein, that can't be right. It has to be one or the other because the synagogue is tearing itself apart. Some people hate each other and families that aren't speaking to each other, and we've practically got fist fights in the parking lot. We're just constantly at each other's throats." And old Mr. Bernstein smiles, nods, and says, "That's the tradition!"

This story captures the essential reality that the act of debate, of differing opinions and practices, is more the tradition than the specific traditions themselves.

For as long as anyone can remember, Jewish tradition has always been this way.

That means you, too, can feel comfortable choosing a pathway that feels supportive and aligned for you, despite what others are doing or claiming is the 'right way,' and that's as authentically Jewish as it gets.

So go ahead and make it your own - that's the tradition!

Some are Good, Generally

Several of the mitzvot feel like plainly good things to do for ourselves and humanity generally: Take care of people experiencing poverty. Love your neighbor as you love yourself. Don't put a stumbling block before the blind. Don't kill. Don't steal.

All of these feel like they're just plain ordinary goodness. Maybe they weren't always.

Structure for Life

Routines, structure, guidance, and discipline can be stabilizing and grounding for all people, especially for children.

In the same way that some people simplify their wardrobe or solidify their routines to minimize decision-making fatigue, mitzvot can help set a structure to follow without having to overthink.

While I am not an advocate of weakening your ability to think critically, simplifying your life can free your capacity to consider other things more deeply.

Mindful Guidance

If performed with intentionality, the mitzvot can also be an excellent tool for bringing deeper awareness and consciousness of the present moment. They can help us bring awareness of the sacredness and remarkability of seemingly unremarkable moments. They provide a built-in way to honor the passing of days, months, and seasons.

CHAPTER 4: WHERE DO WE GET THE 613 MITZVOT FROM IN THE FIRST PLACE?

The Torah (the first five books of the Bible) is the source of all of the mitzvot.

Several rabbis over the millennia have picked through the Torah to itemize the 613 mitzvot. What's interesting is that those lists do not entirely agree.

This implies that there are commandments that are debatable and up for interpretation. Even though everyone seems to agree that 613 is the number, there's a debate about what constitutes them.

The Torah is full of stories you've probably read or heard: The Garden of Eden, Adam and Eve, Noah, Abraham, Moses, and Pharaoh, Israelites wandering in the desert, and the Torah at Mount Sinai.

The Torah begins with those stories and also contains lists of mitzvot. Like the Ten Commandments, for instance.

There are also instances where we need to interpret HOW to understand and apply the mitzvah. The rabbis have their way of understanding these, and those are not always obvious.

For example: 'Do not boil a calf in its mother's milk.'

If you were to take that literally, you'd understand that you should not take a baby cow or a calf from its mother, milk the mother, and boil the baby in its mother's milk. Sounds gruesome, I know.

But that's not how 'the rabbis' have interpreted that verse.

Without getting too complex - they interpret this as a commandment not to eat any meat or dairy together or cook them together. They even add other types of animal meat, like goat, sheep, and even chicken, to the list. It seems like a lot of pretty big stretches to me.

I honor the rabbis and what they contributed. They spoke to the sensibilities of the time and context they lived in. It's time for new paradigms.

Let's talk about Jewish law more in depth.

Rabbinic vs. Torah-Based

In Judaism, there are two categories of mitzvot: those directly written in the Torah and those derived from the rabbis. Classically, these are the Written Torah versus the Rabbinic Laws or De'oraita (divine law) versus De'rabanan (rabbinic law).

In order to avoid transgressing mitzvot (if you see it that way), there are extra laws called harhakot (or mitigators) to create a Siyag L'Torah - literally, 'the fence around the Torah.'

Theoretically, laws that come directly from the Torah are less flexible and more critical, and laws derived by the rabbis are more flexible.

I say theoretically because the way mitzvot are interpreted (by humans) makes a HUGE difference in how they are applied and understood. I'll give a great example below.

One essential thing to realize is how difficult it is to know, with perfect certainty, what the words of the Bible actually mean. Academic critical translations of the Bible are littered in asterisks indicating **meaning of Hebrew uncertain**. If the best and brightest minds aren't sure, it's safe to say there's plenty of room for error and interpretation.

It's very human to seek clarity where there is uncertainty.

Over the centuries, Rabbis have imposed certainty in uncertain and unclear contexts. The abundant interpretations, stories (midrashim), and clarifications by the rabbis over the centuries can sometimes bring unearned clarity to verses that are not clear.

Unearned certainty can be dangerous, especially if we are wrong or bringing our distorted sensibilities and biases into the way we interpret.

If we make moral decisions on how we treat other people based on fuzzy and uncertain language but with an unearned feeling of clarity and certainty, this is especially true.

Most times, leaving things uncertain is the better move and allows for more humility, tentativeness, and flexibility.

Here's an example of how huge a difference interpretation can make:

The Torah commands what you should do with a rebellious, wayward child.

Deuteronomy 21:18-21

18 If a householder has a wayward and defiant son, who does not heed his father or mother and does not obey them even after they discipline him, 19 his father and mother shall take hold of him and bring him out to the elders of his town at the public place of his community. 20 They shall say to the elders of his town, "This son of ours is disloyal and defiant; he does not heed us. He is a glutton and a drunkard." 21 Thereupon, his town's council shall stone him to death. Thus, you will sweep out evil from your midst: all Israel will hear and be afraid.

Basically, if your child is rebellious, you should have them stoned to death. It seems clear.

And yet, no sane person ever followed this mitzvah.

Clearly, humans have a big part to play in enacting the mitzvot or not. Nobody felt this was a good thing to do, so they just ignored it. It's still written there, but nobody follows it.

Mandatory vs. Prohibitive

It is also helpful to know the mitzvot are Positive and Negative, and many of them come in pairs.

Positive commandments say - do this (mitzvot aseh) [מצות עשה].

Negative commandments say - don't do that (mitzvot lo ta'aseh) [מצות לא תעשה].

In some counting systems, there are 248 positive and 365 negative mitzvot. (https://www.britannica.com/topic/mitzvah-Judaism).

A simple example of a mitzvah pairing is:
Love your neighbor as yourself (Positive).
Paired with:
Don't hate your fellow in your heart (Negative).
Do this, don't do that - pretty simple.

Similarly, there's a mitzvah coupling to rest on Shabbat with a mitzvah not to work on the Sabbath.

Bubbe's Brisket: Ignorance and Nostalgia

Ignorance and nostalgia are a potent and sometimes unhelpful combination of how people understand Jewish rituals and customs.

There's a story I call Bubbe's Brisket that helps understand the way these combine to create confusion and sometimes conflict (especially when people are ignorant of the actual mitzvot).

The story goes something like this:

The kids are grown and preparing to host the holiday meal.

They want to prepare all of Bubbe's (grandma's) recipes, especially the brisket!

A few years ago, they got Bubbe to write down her process.

They pull out and follow the recipe.

Everything is going fine, but there's one strange step included:

It says to cut the brisket's end before putting it in the pan.

They argue.

We don't really have to do that.

Yes, we do - that's how Bubbe did it.

She even wrote it down.

It's essential.

That doesn't make any sense! Why?

Maybe it was for the sake of the temple?

Perhaps it was to symbolize leaving the corners of your field for people experiencing poverty.

Either way, that's how Bubbe did it.

We must also do it that way!

Wait - didn't we get Bubbe a new phone?

Why don't we just call and ask?

Hi Bubbe. Happy Holidays! We're making your famous brisket.

There's just one thing.

The recipe says we have to cut the end before we cook it.

You always did that, didn't you?

But we can't figure out why.

Is it essential?

Is there a secret meaning?

Ohh, NO, not at all!

My oven and baking tray were too small to hold the length of the Brisket.

I cut the end so it would fit.

There's no secret meaning.

It was just practical to make it fit in the pan!

If I had a bigger oven and a bigger pan, I wouldn't cut the brisket at all.

Oh! Okay. Our oven and pan fit the whole brisket:

So don't cut it!

~ The End ~

What I love about this story is the way it illustrates how silly and emphatic people can be about the 'right' way - even when they don't know the why of what they're doing.

The kids were fighting over the 'right' way. They ascribe hidden and essential meaning to why she did it that way. Not knowing the practice's origin, they even believe they, too, must do it that way just because she did it that way.

The truth is, it was a practical consideration that is not relevant anymore and has no hidden meaning.

The problem stems from their need for more knowledge (ignorance) about what is essential.

They end up fighting about it, insisting it is done that way, even feeling righteous and correct in doing it that way. While, in truth, they're ignorant and foolish. Too much of Jewish traditional practice is like this.

Non-essential folkways get treated as if they are all-important. People anxiously and neurotically follow them.

Worse yet, people cling to these practices, feeling an unearned sense of superiority or using them to judge themselves or others on whether they got it 'right' or not.

These kinds of things are a source of infighting over nonsense.

We can't just call the rabbis of centuries ago and ask them their practical considerations. But we can, and should, use our common sense to reject (or reinterpret, if possible) any mitzvot we can see as actually harmful, bigoted, sexist, or xenophobic.

In every generation, the law is constantly unfolding and revealing itself. We need to be awake, aware enough, mindful enough, and in tune enough to notice and act accordingly.

CHAPTER 5: HOW DO MODERN MOVEMENTS INTERPRET THE MITZVOT?

We are about to jump into the categories of mitzvot, but before we do that, you should know some varying viewpoints on the mitzvot.

We already talked a little bit about how the commandments come from the Torah.

Judaism is constantly evolving and the debates are ongoing.

It is not as simple as "God Says So."

It's essential to, at a very minimum, discuss how various religious communities generally view the Torah, its authority, and its origin.

Of course, these are generalizations and simplifications, but hopefully, they are helpful tools for your understanding.

Orthodox

This group sees the Torah as being written by God directly. A physical God literally wrote the entire Torah down and handed it over to Moses at Mount Sinai. Every word and commandment is from God directly.

Because of this, nobody can debate anything written in the Torah. We can only discuss how to interpret and enact.

What Does Mitzvah Mean to Them?

In this view, mitzvot are commandments; they are God-given and inflexible.

Knowing and obeying the commandments is essential because God has commanded them.

You can imagine that if you believed in a literal God who physically wrote the commandments, you'd be really careful not to break those rules. And, to make extra sure not to mess up by accident, they developed a whole system of what they call Siyag L'Torah - literally, 'the fence around the Torah.'

A good amount of Orthodox mitzvah observance falls in the 'fence.'

It's like if you knew there was a dangerous cliff, you'd probably try to avoid going near it. If you had to go near the cliff regularly, you'd put up a guardrail or fence to be doubly sure you don't fall off.

Based on the Orthodox understanding that commandments (mitzvot) are the literal words of a literal God, this all makes sense.

Conservative

This group sees the Torah as divinely inspired and written by human beings.

They accept the theory that the Torah was written over different historical periods by various authors and interest groups and compiled together into a single document much later.

This view leaves a lot more room for debate and amendment.

It leaves room to ask - did we make a mistake? Should we reconsider? Did this rule make sense to an ancient society but not anymore?

Basically, the Torah is not directly from the hand of God, and there's more flexibility for re-interpretation and contextualization.

What Does Mitzvah Mean to Them?

This one is a mix. Yes, the Torah is divine, but since it runs through human hands, it's possible we humans get the wrong message from time to time.

As humans grow and advance (hopefully), we find that some of the things we thought were perfectly reasonable 100 or 1000 years ago no longer make any sense.

They take it into their own hands to make corrections and updates.

They're much less worried about disobeying God because they know God and humans work together, and God probably doesn't want us doing things that harm others, are offensive, or don't make any sense from a modern perspective.

The rules are still important but much more flexible.

Let's use one example of how Orthodox and Conservative differ in interpreting a Torah verse:

"Do not lie with a man as one lies with a woman." -Leviticus 18:22

Orthodox would say this prohibits homosexuality.

Conservatives look at this interpretation as clearly in conflict with modern ethical values. They would reinterpret this and restore dignity to homosexual men. Conservative legalists have done this in a variety of ways.

Some say - this refers to a historic non-consensual context of men taking on sex slaves, which no longer exists and certainly does not apply in modern consensual homosexual relationships (Rabbi Bradley Shavit Artson).

I simply say it's merely impossible to lie with a man as you would with a woman because their anatomy is different and eliminate the irrelevant commandment that way.

Either way, you can see that when modern sensibility and ethics come into conflict with mitzvot, the Conservative method is to grapple with, contextualize, and update how we interpret them.

Reform

This group sees the Torah as a classic story of the Israelites and Jewish people, not a Divine work. It's more like a Jewish version of other classic works like Shakespeare.

In this case, the mitzvot are old-timey rules Jews may or may not have lived by.

Mitzvot are loose folkways or cultural traditions we can choose to uphold if we like.

The only ones that would still be relevant are the ones that have made their way into the laws of society because they make sense for all people.

Things like 'don't kill' or 'don't steal' are totally still relevant, but not because God says so.

They're essential because they make sense on a modern ethical and societal level.

Religious rules that are specific to Jewish people, like rules about which foods not to eat or how to observe certain holidays, are customs or guidelines but not commandments, really, and they are definitely not mandatory or divinely required in any meaningful way.

Whereas Orthodox and Conservative Jewish observance of holidays follow the Jewish calendar and are inflexible, Reform Jews may approximate the dates of Jewish holidays for convenience. They might just observe on a day when everyone can be in town or push it to a weekend so it doesn't interrupt their lives. Orthodox and Conservative observe strictly on the day the holiday falls on the calendar.

All of The Movements

The truth is, whether you admit it or not, humans have always had a hand in the interpretation of the mitzvot.

You might believe it's all from God, but if you're really being honest with yourself, you'd admit human beings are the ones deciding and even updating how we do and don't follow the commandments.

It is fascinating that honest and aware Orthodox legal interpreters acknowledge this truth.

They are often more bound and limited by the customs of their communities, 'the fences,' and Bubbe's brisket followers' opinions than by the actual law itself.

They hope to be guided by God in their discernment - that their words and interpretations bring more goodness, love, and divine expression into the world and not cause harm.

Beyond What Exists

Beyond the written laws, 613 is representative of a beckoning to tune in to the Divine in every moment.

It's an invitation to tune into your Divine spark and all its aspirations, to the visions it pulls you toward, whether or not it makes sense to you and your rational mind.

Being in touch with the 613 mitzvot requires being deeply rooted in each moment as it arises.

Mitzvot are beyond any written code. They're subjective. They're moment to moment. They can only be discovered, never preserved. At best, we can provide a heuristic model to help people learn to recognize and trust their intuitive knowledge and the unfolding mitzvot.

"The close-minded notion that God communicated...but then fell forever mute has contributed to many generations of deafness to the divine. Those who recognize that "God is still speaking" gain access not only to ancient wisdom but modern revelations as well." - Leena B. Brown

CHAPTER 6: SEVEN TYPES OF MITZVOT

In the following section, I'll break down the major categories of Mitzvot. Hopefully, by simplifying these, you'll have a 'Birds Eye view' of the general landscape. This way, you can decide to explore any one of these categories more thoroughly. Here's a list if you want to skip around:

1) Shabbat, Holidays, and Festivals 2) Kosher & Diet 3) Ethics 4) Divine Oneness & No Idolatry 5) Rituals 6) Uncut Gems 7) Irrelevant or Offensive

1) Shabbat, Holidays, and Festivals

These are the rules for how to observe Shabbat, Holidays, and Festivals.

The basic mitzvah for all of the above is to make these days restful. The idea is to make them unique and not treat them like every other productive day. These days are an invitation to be mindful of how wonderful the world is already without us needing to do anything to enhance it.

In order for these days to be genuinely restful, you have to prepare. It's like if you were to go camping on a whim versus if you are well prepared and packed. It's fun if you're ready. It's probably not so fun if you aren't.

The Torah itself is relatively minimalistic in regard to Shabbat restrictions, but the rabbis created a very in-depth and complex system of rules. The rabbis used the list of tasks (Melachot) required to build the traveling ark (Mishkan). There are 39 of these melachot - they range from building a fire, planting, winnowing, dying fabrics, and straining items.

Since the discovery of electricity, there has been a debate about whether to treat it as fire (which is prohibited) or whether it is something else, something new and therefore permitted for use.

On holidays, we're allowed to cook. But not on Shabbat.

Want to know what the 'rules' are for how to observe Passover, Sukkot, Rosh Hashanah, or Yom Kippur? There are all kinds of mitzvot about what to do and not to do. Some of the origins of these mitzvot come from the Torah directly, and others are rituals supplemented and interpreted by the rabbis throughout the centuries. There are also a bunch of customs that have evolved separately from the mitzvot but that many people would consider almost as or even more important than the classical mitzvot (of the Bubbe's Brisket variety).

Popular holidays like Hanukkah and Purim are not in the Torah at all - both were added to Jewish observance later in time. They have mitzvot but are completely rabbinically derived.

Each of the special days has unique practices.

There is a mitzvah to hear the Shofar blown on Rosh Hashanah.

Yom Kippur has a list of rabbinic mitzvot.

There is a mitzvah prohibiting eating Hametz (traditionally interpreted as leavened products or bread) on Passover.

On Sukkot, there is a mitzvah of dwelling, or sitting, in a temporary hut.

The holidays are tied to the agricultural and seasonal cycle and always fall into their specific season.

2) Kosher and Diet

There are kosher guidelines that clearly come straight from the Torah and an entire rabbinic enterprise of modern kosher, which is many steps removed from the original Torah mitzvot.

Kosher vs. Unkosher Animals, Fish, Birds

The Torah lists guidelines for which foods we can eat. See Chapter 11 of Leviticus if you want to see more.

Mammals require a split hoof and must chew their cud. Some of the animals mentioned explicitly as unkosher are camels, hyraxes, hares, and pigs.

Some examples of split-hoofed-cud-chewers are cows, sheep, goats, and deer.

Water animals must have fins and scales. Tuna, yellowtail, tilapia, flounder, carp, herring, trout, whitefish, and salmon are among those that have fins and scales.

Some of the water animals that would not be kosher are lobster, crab, shrimp, crawfish, oysters, clams, eels, sharks, dolphins, whales, and other shellfish.

The list of prohibited birds is lengthy: eagles, kites, osprey, kestrels, vultures, ravens, ostriches, jays, sparrow hawks, owls, bats, starlings, magpies, storks, herons, hoopoe, and similar birds. Many of the unkosher birds listed are predatory or scavengers.

We can eat the more domestic types of birds: chickens, pigeons, ducks, geese, and turkeys, for example.

When it comes to insects, we may not eat insects that fly and have four legs. Nor anything that creeps on its belly, like snakes.

Animals that creep on the ground are not kosher, such as weasels, mice, toads, hedgehogs, chameleons, lizards, snails, and moles. However, we may eat red, yellow, spotted grey, and white locusts.

We may also not eat animals that we find dead.

Meat, Milk, and Pareve

In the previous section, we covered the different types of animals that are considered kosher. The rabbis considered birds meat.

Fish are pareve - which means not meat and not dairy - alongside any fruits, veggies, fungi, and grains.

Milk and dairy products of any kosher animal are also kosher.

Another element of kosher is avoiding mixing meat and milk.

Three times, the Torah states, "Do not boil a calf in its mother's milk." While this might seem to literally indicate we should not be cruel and take a nursing mother cow or goat's milk, slaughter the calf, and then cook it in their milk, the rabbis have interpreted this to mean we should not cook, warm, or combine meat and dairy in any way.

The rabbis also constructed an elaborate guideline system for what to do if you make a mistake and don't want to throw out the whole dish.

Kosher Slaughter and Animal Cruelty

There is a mitzvah not to torture animals and to treat them as humanely as possible.

To this end, traditionally, all the warm-blooded kosher mammals and birds listed above must also undergo shehitah (kosher slaughter), which involves a flawlessly sharp knife, a special blessing, swiftly cutting the blood supply to the brain, and inspection of the animal to ensure it doesn't have any blemishes, then, in most cases, salting (to remove blood) before being eaten.

The idea behind the flawlessly sharp knife is to cause the least amount of suffering in the animal as possible in the course of their slaughter. I'll say more about this in the Ethics section on animals. Specific methods come from rabbinic interpretations and traditions.

Pots, Pans, and Dishes

The rabbis dove pretty deep into extending kosher to pots, pans, dishes, and utensils used to cook and serve. Basically, there's an elaborate rabbinic 'science' system of rules for how meat, dairy, or non-kosher-ness does or doesn't transfer into and out of different types of materials (metal, glass, wood, and ceramics).

It Is Subjective

They say if you want to make your Jewish life more manageable, learn more about Kosher laws, and if you're going to make it harder, learn Shabbat laws.

That's because the rabbis extrapolate lots of the kosher laws. There are also lots of loopholes and concepts to help account for innocent mistakes and curb food waste and expense.

The same food item could be deemed kosher and not kosher, depending on context. It could be Kosher for someone under financial strain and not kosher for a person who could easily afford to purchase new and unquestionably kosher food.

3) Ethics

These are the most universally relevant and applicable, no matter where you fall on the Orthodox <—> Reform spectrum. Some would say these are Judaism's significant contributions to modern society. We could probably apply some of these principles to make the world a better place.

Treatment of Others (Interpersonal)

One of the pillars of Judaism is treating others well. One core mitzvah is to Love your fellow as yourself. It appears eight times in the Torah. The rabbis later argue that there is no greater mitzvah.

It is connected closely with Do not hate your fellow in your heart. The Torah tells us that carrying hatred in our hearts without either releasing it or expressing our boundaries to the person who hurt us goes against the laws of Judaism.

Keeping your vows is another less obvious way we honor one another.

The mitzvot in this category extend to all people and relationships with parents, spouses, children, people in financial need, employees, fellow humans, older people, clients, widows, orphans, and animals.

There is also a prohibition against oppressing strangers (those less fortunate than you), which appears three dozen times in various forms.

There are also special mitzvot for honoring our parents, spouses, children, people in financial need, employees, fellow humans, elderly, clients, and animals.

Mitzvot like these are the justification for canceling out some of the mitzvot found in the Torah that violate or compete with this tenant.

As we evolve and progress as a society, some mitzvot that were once widely accepted with no resistance come into conflict with the mitzvot that commands us not to hate, to love, and never to oppress others.

I'll say more about that in section 7 below, entitled: Irrelevant or Offensive.

Business

Jewish law recognizes that business and livelihood are a significant part of life.

These mitzvot aim to ensure fair and ethical practices in the business world or marketplace.

These are rules on how to treat our employees and customers fairly, how to make sure you aren't harming others while making a living, and generally being honest and upright in how you represent your products.

There are rules for how to draft contracts, etc.

The following are some of the mitzvot related to how we ethically and honestly conduct business:

- Pay Your People On Time - Don't Hold Wages: "Do not hold back the wages of a hired hand overnight." (Leviticus 19:13) and "Do not abuse a laborer who is destitute and needy." (Deuteronomy 24:14-15)
- No deception: "When you sell anything to your neighbor or buy anything from your neighbor, you shall not deceive one another."(Leviticus 25:14)
- No false weights or measures: "You shall not falsify measures of length, weight, or capacity. You shall have an honest balance, an honest weight, an honest ephah, and an honest hin."(Leviticus 19:35-36)

Sexual Limitations (Prohibited Relations)

Judaism supports sexual intimacy with some limits. There is a positive mitzvah of having children (Genesis 1:28 says, "Be fruitful and multiply"), but most of the mitzvot about sex are negative.

Incest and close family relationships are prohibited. The following is a list of many people we are explicitly forbidden to have sex with found in Leviticus 18: mother/father, stepmother/father, sister/brother, half-sister/brother, granddaughter/son, half-brother/sister, aunt/uncle (direct or via marriage), daughter/son-in-law, brother's wife, sister's husband. And, no sex with animals.

I'll say more about the traditional and new Jewish interpretations of same-gender sex in the Irrelevant and Offensive section below.

Animals

Judaism definitely sees animal welfare as being important based on a mitzvah forbidding unnecessary cruelty to animals (Tza'ar Ba'alei Chayim).

While we are allowed to eat meat, we are not allowed to be abusive to animals or cause them needless suffering.

Kosher slaughter is an ancient attempt to cause the least amount of suffering to the animal as possible in the process of killing them. For many years, kosher slaughter was probably the highest standard in humanely taking the lives of animals we eat.

However, with modern advances in animal welfare research, it's arguable that there are now quicker, more efficient, and higher, more humane ways to slaughter animals than kosher.

In time, Judaism may adapt its requirements to those modern innovations.

The following is a list of some more mitzvot related to ethical treatment of animals:

* Animals rest on Shabbat just as humans do (Exodus 20:10).
* Do not muzzle an Ox while it works in the field (Deuteronomy 25:4). Just as a chef should be able to eat and

taste while they cook, animals should be allowed to graze while they work.

- Do not yolk animals of different species together to plow a field (Deuteronomy 22:10). Otherwise, they'll hurt each other.
- Don't kill an animal on the same day as its young (Leviticus 22:28). It's cruel.
- Send a mother bird away before taking eggs from her nest (Deuteronomy 22:6-7) lest she be extra distressed watching.

Clearly, animals are not an afterthought in Jewish ethical considerations; they are important, and how we treat them is important.

People In Need: Charity and Justice

Another category of mitzvot is charity (tzedakah) and repairing the world (tikkun olam). The word tzedakah literally means justice or righteousness. The mitzvah of giving of surplus and taking care of others is part of how we make the world a better place. It's so crucial that rabbis of the Talmud have said charity is equal to all the other commandments combined.

Judaism is both spiritual and practical. The Torah gives Jewish people an aspirational commandment of eradicating poverty, that "there should be no poor among you." (Deuteronomy 15:4) And, "If there is a needy person among you...do not harden your heart...Rather, you must open your hand and lend whatever is sufficient to meet the need." (Deuteronomy 15:7-8) In the event that we have not accomplished the task of eliminating poverty, we must respond and help. Mitzvot command our communal and individual responsibility to feed, cloth, and shelter those who need help.

No matter how much or little we have, we are all encouraged to and required to give. There is always someone who we can help.

Help doesn't always need to be financial.

We can also give our time, energy, and expertise to teach skills that help someone become independent. Even sharing a smile or encouragement is a form of giving.

Beyond charity, some are in need of companionship or who are ill and would benefit from human interaction.

The Torah also emphasizes the mitzvah of lending money without interest (Leviticus 25:36-37 and Deuteronomy 23:20). Many Jewish communities have a free loan society offering interest-free loans. Contributing to one of these organizations is an easy way to fulfill this commandment.

4) Divine Oneness and No Idolatry

This combination is central to Judaism. First, there's only one God. Second, don't idolize anything else — not a person, animal, place, object, force, or spirit.

The Shma is one of Judaism's central prayers. It's almost certainly part of B-Mitzvah, and it's the sentence converts proclaim when they become Jewish. It says, "Listen Israel, God is ours, God is ONE." (Deuteronomy 6:4). The emphasis is on oneness.

On Atheism

I'm not here to argue. These are just my honest thoughts.

I think being an 'atheist' is just as absurd as being a 'believer.' What I'm saying is that I don't think there's a way to prove OR disprove God's existence irrefutably.

Whether you believe or DON'T believe, you're equally sure about something that nobody can really 100% prove. Both take a leap of faith in order to be 'sure,' and neither can prove their belief for certain.

To be agnostic is to admit being unsure.

It means we don't know, but we're open to the possibility. Being agnostic is saying you're not 100% convinced either way.

To me, agnosticism is a much more logical place to stand than atheism, and being agnostic falls into alignment with the mitzvah of not having a different God or idolizing/serving false deities.

It's very Jewish.

Torah and the Jewish tradition are much more concerned with NOT idolizing or serving false gods than they are with convincing you of anything else.

I am also personally less interested in convincing people to believe in God's existence. I'm much more serious about ensuring we're not worshiping something or someone false.

5) Rituals

Day-to-day: Ritual Objects, Blessings, and Prayer

The rabbis came up with an elaborate system of prayers and blessings for nearly everything and every time of day.

We utilize these to bring mindful gratitude to our daily lives, acknowledging how fortunate we are and connecting the goodness that comes into our lives without our doing anything at all.

Some Jewish ritual objects serve to remind us of the mitzvot and can also help retrain our mindfulness of the sacred. These are a few:

Tzitzit

These are fringe strings on the corners of the prayer shawls, known as a Talit, usually worn for prayers. Some people wear them all day. "They shall make for themselves a fringe [tzitzit]" (Numbers 15:38).

Tefillin

Also known as phylacteries, they are a set of two leather boxes and leather straps containing parchment scrolls with the Shma and a few other verses. Traditionally, they are worn during weekday morning prayers. "Bind them as a sign on your hands and as a symbol between your eyes" (Deuteronomy 6:8).

Mezuza

A small box containing a parchment of the Shma traditionally affixed to most doorposts in the home. They are a reminder of Exodus from Egypt, a central Jewish theme highlighted in Passover and throughout the year. It is also a reminder that the Divine accompanies us in all spaces. "Inscribe them on the doorposts of your house and on your gates" (Deuteronomy 6:9).

Blessings

Modern mindfulness, spirituality, psychology, and neuroscience have all deeply embraced the power of gratitude to shift and improve our lives. Long before this, Judaism developed a vast system of blessings for almost every activity we take part in on a daily basis.

There are blessings for the most basic human needs and experiences, like drinking water or using the restroom.

There are blessings for the foods we eat, pleasant smells, and having a working/healthy body.

There's even one for seeing a rainbow, hearing thunder, or hearing good or bad news.

At its core, the Jewish tradition is about recognizing, acknowledging, and praising the good in our lives.

King David said 100 blessings a day; each day, he looked for 100 things to be grateful for.

Imagine going through life searching for the good.

That's a powerful way of directing your attention and training yourself to be mindful of how sweet life is.

One explicit mitzvah is from Deuteronomy 8:10, which teaches, "and you will eat and be satisfied and bless the Divine," which gives us the responsibility to be grateful after we've eaten and feel satiated. What a fantastic way to practice gratitude on a daily, regular basis for our sustenance.

Below is the basic traditional formula for blessings, but feel free to adapt it to what feels right for you.

בָּרוּךְ אַתָּה יְיָ, אֱלֹהֵינוּ מֶלֶךְ הָעוֹלָם...

Transliterated: Baruch Atta Adonai Eloheinu Melech HaOlam ...

Blessed are You, Divine, Sustainer of All Life in the Universe, for...

Here are some other types of blessings that you could find ways to incorporate into your life:

Blessings for:

nice smells,

the foods you eat,

our healthy, working bodies and senses,

and for witnessing nature's wonders.

Blessings are a great way to stay connected with gratitude for all the excellent parts of life and, if you were so inclined, to thank the Divine for those being part of reality.

Prayer

Over 2000 years ago, Judaism transitioned from an animal sacrifice system to a prayer and ritual system.

Rabbis adopted the sacrificial system's timing of 3 daily offerings and additional offerings during holidays and Shabbat (Mussaf) to create a formal prayer structure to mirror the sacrificial system.

As such, traditionally, there are three formal prayer time windows per day and specific prayer suggestions/requirements for each of those times (evening, morning, and afternoon - or Arvieet, Shacharit, and Mincha).

Rather than see these as a requirement, I see them as a series of daily opportunities to recenter yourself.

One of the worst things a human can experience is feeling alone with their struggles. The Jewish antidote to this is gathering in the community and reaching out to God.

We embrace and recognize the human need to express and share our struggle, to reach out for help, and to ask for good for ourselves, our loved ones, and all of humanity.

It is beautiful that if you're struggling or mourning the loss of a loved one, you can find community prayer sessions multiple times a day to join.

To be totally honest, the reality is probably less flowery than I'm trying to portray it.

In my experience, the types of communities that prioritize gathering for daily prayer are the types that feel communally and individually required to do so.

So what you find is a core of people who show up regularly, out of duty, and speed through the requirements.

Who am I to say what kind of intent they pour into the prayer or not?

Paradoxically, it seems that when people pray from a sense of obligation rather than from a sense of inspiration, need, and desire to connect with God, they end up seeking ways to 'get through it' as quickly as possible.

There's not really a whole lot of intent, or at least, it doesn't feel that way.

It is, however, a distinct flavor of service.

If you're looking to connect with other humans, you'll find that opportunity either before prayers begin or after they are over. And, if you're looking to connect with God, you'll probably do better at a yoga or mindfulness-type gathering.

Nevertheless, the Jewish prayer system and its timing invite us to stay connected and express our heartfelt prayers whenever we need to.

Weekly

Shabbat, the holiest Jewish holiday, is every single Friday night through Saturday night. The mitzvah of Shabbat is to "Remember Shabbat and make it holy." (Exodus 20:8) and to "Safeguard Shabbat and make it holy." (Deuteronomy 5:12).

It's a day to set aside and remember, unlike other days of the week. If we treat it intentionally, it can be an incredible opportunity to relax, recover, and soak in all the natural goodness of this Universe on a weekly basis.

Monthly

Every new moon, there are special Jewish prayers and rituals.

Beyond those prayers, you could use the new moon or full moon as a time to check in, replenish yourself, or just charge your crystals in the moonlight (or whatever people do with crystals on full moons).

Seasonal

Jewish holidays fall in specific seasons of the year, tied to the agricultural rhythms of Israel.

The high holidays and Sukkot are always in the fall. Hanukkah is always in the winter. Passover is always in the Spring.

We can use Jewish holidays to not only tune into the specific Jewish stories and rituals of those holidays but also to stay in tune with the natural seasonal rhythms of the year.

6) Uncut Gems

The Jewish legal system is remarkable in its thoroughness. The methods and guidelines here could be constructive for navigating complex and contentious circumstances in life.

There are mitzvot for how to appoint judges, who can be considered a witness, many rules to protect against conflicts of interest, and laws to ensure the rule of law applies equally to rich and poor.

That said, a good chunk of mitzvot do not seem to make sense in any logical way. One of these is the prohibition of mixing wool and linen (Shatnez). While there may be explanations for why these types of mitzvot exist, there is no way to really know what their purpose is.

It's simple to explain and agree it is best for society that we don't kill or steal. The function of kosher laws is less clear. Can we come up with reasons and guesses? Yes, for sure. And we do. But, if we're really being honest, we don't know. We're just guessing.

Just because we don't currently understand things doesn't mean we couldn't eventually gain clarity. I call these uncut gems because maybe one day we will understand the relevance and value of this category of mitzvot. Who knows?

7) Irrelevant or Offensive

Temple, Sacrifice, and Israel-Related

Of the total 613 mitzvot listed in the Torah, many are related to the ancient sacrificial system, which doesn't exist today.

The Chafetz Chayim, Rabbi Israel Meir Kagan, says we can only follow 271 of the total 613 mitzvot.

Any modern application of these is, at best, metaphoric unless you're trying to bring back the sacrificial system.

You could extrapolate meaning from them - by all means, go for it. They could fall into the above category of uncut gems, too.

In this category are laws that only apply to Cohanim (priests) and Levites, rules on what clothes the priests wear, how they behave, eligibility for service in the temple, how to sprinkle sacrificial blood, and a whole lot more irrelevant things like that.

There are also a bunch of agricultural laws that only apply within the state of Israel (usually to do with sabbatical years). People uphold the Israel-based agricultural laws today in modern Israel.

Rooted In Phobia or Oppression

One of the central mitzvot of Judaism is treating all beings with love, respect, and dignity. As a rule, whenever a mitzvah arises that competes with this, love and preserving human dignity are always more important.

As society evolves and progresses, cultural and societal norms shift and ethical considerations change.

Any mitzvah that violates Love Your Fellow must be canceled out and rejected. It's a mitzvah to make necessary changes whether the mitzvah is xenophobic, oppressive, misogynistic, or homophobic - or in any way insensitive.

I'll give three examples:

Slavery has been considered immoral globally for at least a few hundred years. The Torah has many mitzvot related to the way to keep a slave, but as we have adapted to the modern day, we no longer permit enslaving people.

Women were not considered equal to men for centuries. It was accepted and commonplace for women not to be permitted to own property, vote, or even apply for a credit card! Society changed. Most of the world has progressed to believe women should have equal rights to men. Any of the Jewish mitzvot that stand to oppress or diminish the respect of women are no longer valid.

The last example is the cancellation of any of the prohibitions on same-gender sexuality, as those clearly oppress and diminish their human dignity and right to express themselves and live their lives with dignity.

CHAPTER 7: NOW WHAT?

Read the List of the 613

For an essential list of the entire 613 mitzvot, with no commentary, you can check out either:

Sefer Ha'Mitzvot (online) (https://www.sefaria.org/ Sefer_HaMitzvot?tab=contents)

or, for hard copies,

The Concise Book of Mitzvot or The Taryag Mitzvos.

For a complete list with more explanation, check out the book Sefer Ha'Chinuch (entirely online) (https://www.sefaria.org/ Sefer_HaChinukh?tab=contents). It tracks the mitzvot according to the weekly Torah portion from Genesis through the end of Deuteronomy.

Try One That Resonates, One That You Are Neutral on, and One You Can't Understand.

My colleague Rabbi Gary Ezra Oren gave me this wise suggestion when I was interested in deepening my relationship with Jewish practice.

He suggested choosing a practice that resonates with you. Something easy that you feel yourself gravitating toward.

Pick a second that you don't feel any particular way about.

Lastly, pick a mitzvah to practice that feels like a stretch. Either it makes no sense to you or actively makes you a bit uncomfortable. Obviously, nobody is asking you to do anything that offends you.

Do those for a few months and see how it goes. You might be surprised to find that the way you feel about them shifts over time.

Notice How or If It Helps You

This is worth repeating.

When you plant a garden, you envision the results you want: fruit, vegetables, herbs, and flowers. The same is true of spiritual practice.

What result do you want? A calmer, more peaceful life? More ability to focus? A feeling of connection with others or with the Divine? An ability to feel more mindful in your daily activities?

It's essential to set out knowing what result you want. Then, later, you can check and see if it accomplished the intended result.

The test of all spiritual practice should be how it eventually impacts your life. Does it make a difference? Do you feel better? Worse? Does it help you?

Some practices take time to make a difference, so hold off on evaluating their impact until you've had time to practice them. But always keep an eye on whether or not the practices are helpful to you.

Dear 83-Year-Old Man

The conversation with the 83-year-old man serves as a powerful reminder of the disconnect many feel between the ritual of the B-Mitzvah and its deeper meaning. His frustration reflects a broader concern that, too often, we focus on the surface-level rituals rather than the transformative spiritual potential these moments hold.

The B-Mitzvah ceremony should not just be about memorizing Hebrew or performing a social obligation—it should be about awakening to the deeper wisdom of Judaism and the personal growth that can come from engaging with its teachings.

By revitalizing the way we approach mitzvot and the B-Mitzvah process, we can reconnect with the true purpose of these traditions, using them as tools for spiritual growth and meaningful living.

Just as a garden requires intention and care to grow, so too does a life lived in alignment with Jewish wisdom. With the right focus, the B-Mitzvah can become a milestone in a lifelong journey of self-discovery, connection, and fulfillment.

Know and Follow Your Intuition

It's not about the 613 laws but about following your inner light.

It's about knowing how to follow your God-given inner compass. It's about learning to trust the part of you that discerns what's right and good for you and all life.

We are all One.

Following God's mitzvot is inseparable from following your intuition. Your intuition doesn't need to make sense to anyone besides you. Honestly, it doesn't even need to make logical sense to you.

When you clearly feel called, and only you can know that calling is, it's your Mitzvah - your commandment - to follow in that direction. No matter how scary, no matter how confusing, no matter how counter-logical it seems.

Want more? Connect with your local rabbi or Rav Ariel to deepen your learning.

ACKNOWLEDGMENTS

Thank you to Rabbi Jeff Roth and Brian Arnell at the Awakened Heart Project for your administrative and emotional support, not just in this project but for the past decade-plus.

Thank you to Madeleine and Kendal for your edits, and thank you to Shea for your help formatting the cover.

Hannah, thank you for your encouragement and love.

I am very grateful to my wise teachers, Rabbis Bradley Shavit Artson, Elliot Dorff, Cheryl Peretz, Stewart Vogel, Elie Kaplan Spitz, Mimi Feigelson, Aryeh Cohen, Aaron Alexander, and Yehudah Hausman.

Thank you to my grandfather, Sabba Yosef - for wrapping me in your tallit and rubbing my back during services.

I'm also indebted to all the ancestors, blood and spiritual, who either physically helped create my DNA or who give me the guidance and strength to persist and thrive in service of something greater than myself. My wish is to be an ancestor who also helped pave the way for a better path.

I feel incredibly blessed to have made this offering a reality. Thank you, Source of All, for all the good I know, for all the good I couldn't possibly know, and for all the good to come.